"Do you ever tu[...]ls you to eat a healthy d[...]rogram? You know you need to do those things, but perhaps what you are lacking is a timely or compelling *why* to fuel your motivation. If this is how you regard the scriptural exhortation to humble yourself, the pages that follow will help you tune in to many timely and compelling *whys*. *Humbled* will give you a new perspective of the myriad of ways that God works in your life."

Gloria Furman, author of *Labor with Hope* and *A Tale of Two Kings*

"David is once again a very reliable guide. He is careful with Scripture and always clear and pastoral. In this short book, he takes an important piece of humility—'humble yourself'—and lets us delight in being a little smaller and a little less special."

Ed Welch, author, counselor, and faculty member at CCEF

"Humility is a counter-intuitive invitation to holy bliss and human flourishing—to receive with gratitude our creatureliness and to live so that the glory of God shines through us. This book from David Mathis is a powerful and concise treatment of an indispensable virtue."

Trevin Wax, vice president for research and resource development at the North American Mission Board and visiting professor at Wheaton College; author of *Rethink Your Self*, *This Is Our Time*, and *Counterfeit Gospels*

"The Bible's call to humility is clear and yet few of us pursue it with the diligence of which the Bible speaks. What David Mathis has given us in this book is a brief, clear, sober, and most importantly humble call for the pursuit of the uniquely human virtue of humility to the glory of God. Humility does not come naturally. Nothing that glorifies Christ ever does. David Mathis reminds us that it is the pleasure of the Holy Spirit to direct us in humility and thus make us more like Christ, who amazingly humbled himself. This is a quick read, yet long-lasting and encouraging in its impact."

Anthony Carter, lead pastor of East Point Church; author of *Running from Mercy* and *Black and Reformed*

"Although humility is a quality many of us admire, very few of us understand its significance or desire to pursue it personally. In *Humbled*, David Mathis has contributed a work that I believe will unlock an essential teaching of Scripture that God opposes the proud but gives grace to the humble. I am so grateful for how David uses Scripture faithfully to show us why humility is to be desired, and yet he is realistic with the difficult work that must take place to produce humility in our hearts. It is truly a work that is initiated by God but one that we participate in. David gives practical advice on how to position ourselves for this deep work of God in our lives and reminds us that humility is at the heart of the gospel."

Afshin Ziafat, lead pastor, Providence Church, Frisco, Texas; council member, The Gospel Coalition

"*Humbled* is a small but mighty book, packed with biblical wisdom and countercultural insight. Mathis is incisive, eloquent, and rigorously faithful to Scripture. I can't recommend this book enough, especially to my fellow young Christians."

Jaquelle Crowe Ferris, author, *This Changes Everything*; cofounder, TheYoungWriter.com

"David Mathis serves us all by pointing us to a topic we can't think too much about. I give much of my time to leading conversations about race and racism. The number one thing I wish we all had more of in the conversation is humility. Mathis reminds us that God is the One who humbles us. Read this book to learn how you should respond to His merciful, humbling hand—however heavy it may seem."

Isaac Adams, assistant pastor, Capitol Hill Baptist Church; founder, United? We Pray

"Biblical, insightful, and convicting, *Humbled* is a fresh reminder to receive the humbling of God as a call to become more Christlike. In our world of self-promotion, Mathis challenges us to heed the lessons of humility woven throughout Scripture and welcome the uncomfortable work of God who brings all things for our good and His glory."

Vaneetha Risner, author of *Walking Through Fire: A Memoir of Loss and Redemption*

"This book offers sweet relief for those being humbled and a clear path of preparation for those in more clement seasons. Mathis weaves insights from the stories of kings in the Bible, culminating in the humility of the King of kings. This powerful book would make an excellent study for Sunday school, small groups, or leadership teams."

Gerrit Dawson, senior pastor, First Presbyterian Church of Baton Rouge

"In *Humbled*, Mathis has once again given the church a resource that not only engages the heart and mind, but is also clearly purposed to equip our hands for daily Christian living. This work feels as timely as it does timeless. David is faithful to let the word of God do the heavy lifting as he clarifies, at times with great nuance, the purpose and process behind the command to 'humble yourself.' With every passing chapter, I felt a growing excitement at the blessing that could reach my own heart, home, and city if God were to do this kind of Humbled work in me."

Matt Bradner, staff development, Campus Outreach

humbled

Welcoming the Uncomfortable
Work of God

David Mathis

BHPUBLISHING.COM

To Megan

Contents

Introduction

God humbled the whole world in 2020.

First China, then Italy, England, and all of Europe. Then, the purported "greatest nation in the world," at least in many American eyes, was humbled as much, if not more, than any other. I can't speak for other countries, but as an American, I remember wave after humbling wave, and the ripples haven't yet subsided.

Here it all seemed to turn on a dime. Coronavirus in China was back-page news. Then, seemingly all of a sudden, fever pitch. And you know it's serious when Americans cancel a major sporting event, like the NCAA basketball tournament. Then the NBA season. And Major League Baseball sent everyone home from Spring Training.

States instituted lockdowns, forced quarantines, and mask mandates in varying degrees. Idol after American idol was postponed and cancelled. We were awash in uncertainty and wild speculation. Even the seeming experts were out of their league. We were waking afresh to how little we really know, how little control we have, and how fragile our lives and world can be.

As we struggled to wade through the new avalanche of enigmas unleashed by COVID-19, the death of George Floyd (not far from my own home), and the subsequent protests and riots, in Minneapolis and beyond, brought additional waves of humbling. Not only about the present. Now more questions about the past. And what will this all mean for our future?

Of course, the humbling didn't stay nice and hermetically sealed off to 2020. Just days into the new year, as Congress gathered to count the electoral votes, a mob breached barriers to push onto the grounds, and some into the halls, of the Capitol itself, some snapping selfies, but some armed, seemingly ready to unleash shocking violence if given the chance.

Before a watching world, this was yet another humbling event for the United States, a nation that puts itself forward to the world as a beacon of democracy and a model of order, domestic tranquility, and the peaceful transition of power. The nation that offers to help other nations hold peaceful elections struggled with the aftermath of its own.

But for most of us, the humbling of nations through novel viruses, civil unrest, and threats of insurrection pales in comparison to the humbling circumstances that often devastate our own lives. For the vast majority of us, the daily news and its catalogue of humblings, mild and severe, touch our little lives very little.

Our most earth-shattering humblings are often known by only friends and family, even as the edifice of our lives can feel like it's crashing down. The loss of a job. The loss of a child. The loss of a spouse. Divorce. A terrible accident. The exposure of some private

Our most earth-shattering humblings are often known by only friends and family, even as the edifice of our lives can feel like it's crashing down.

sin, whether sexual, financial, substance abuse, or some other embarrassment.

It could be the corrective words, however gracious, of a spouse or close friend.

It could be finding ourselves newly laid bare before our God in daily meditation as his Word does its wonderful and uncomfortable work on us.

How many of us have found that God himself, through the Scriptures and the power of his Spirit, not only gives us spiritual life by feeding our souls but also exposes, and cuts painfully toward, the cancers of sin within us:

> The word of God is living and active, sharper than any two-edged sword, piercing to the division of soul and of spirit, of joints and of marrow, and discerning the thoughts and intentions of the heart. And no creature is hidden from his sight, but all are naked and exposed to the eyes of him to whom we must give account. (Heb. 4:12–13)

Humbled. To live in this world, fallen as it is, and sinners as we are, is to be humbled. It's only a matter of time.

Only the grace of God gives us breathing room between our many and memorable humblings. God could undo us daily if he chose. We'd be fully deserving of it. Yet in his kindness and patience, he unfolds our lives as far more than a series of humblings. We experience far more days of grace and joy than we deserve.

However, our God is not so unloving as to let us parade ever on through this life without the severe mercy of his humbling hand. It descends, often without warning. We're caught off guard. It hurts to be humbled. We do not want it. We would pray, like Jesus, for the cup to pass. But it is here, as we each kneel in our own Gethsemanes before our Father, that he does his genuine humbling work in us—on his terms, not the ones we would choose. In his timing, not ours.

How do I humble myself? In one sense, it's a question Scripture prompts us to ask, because we are commanded to humble ourselves. "Seek humility"

(Zeph. 2:3). "Put on . . . humility" (Col. 3:12). "Have . . . a humble mind" (1 Pet. 3:8). "Humble yourselves before the Lord" (James 4:10). "Humble yourselves . . . under the mighty hand of God" (1 Pet. 5:6). Okay, then, how do I humble myself? Yet this could be a question we approach in a quintessentially, unhumbled American kind of way, assuming we can just up and do it. *Just tell me how. I'll get it done.*

In contrast to this attitude, the humble-self theme in Scripture turns our human instincts and assumptions upside down. Yes, this is indeed a biblical directive. And at the same time, it's not something we can just up and do. We cannot humble ourselves by our own bootstraps.

We cannot humble ourselves by our own bootstraps.

When we trace out this language of self-humbling going back to Exodus and the lowly Moses standing before Pharaoh, mighty and arrogant, and through the history of Israel's kings (especially in 2 Chronicles), to the exile and restoration, and into the ministry of Jesus and the words of the apostles, we find this to be a humbling theme indeed.

We humans are not the drivers of our own humility. Our God designs the humbling way in which he forges the virtue of humility. He takes the initiative. He acts first. Our humility happens on his terms. He sees. He knows. He moves, with sovereign, omnipotent, meticulous care. He is intimately engaged with his created world and with each of his creatures. He is the one who humbles us with his mighty hand, and when his humbling hand descends and we're cut to our knees or flat on the ground, then the question comes to us: Will you *humble yourself* and embrace God's humbling hand, or will you try to fight back?

Will you receive his humbling providences, or attempt to explain them away?

Will you soften to him in humility, or harden with pride?

True self-humbling is not our initiative, but it does require our doing as we learn to welcome the uncomfortable work of God.

Is there anything we can do to seek humility, or are we simply left to wait for God's next severe mercy to humble us? God has given means of his grace to pursue, and to build habits in light of, so that when his humbling hand does descend again, we might be ready to receive it as what it is, embrace him in faith, and genuinely humble ourselves in response to his uncomfortable work.

This short book is a modest study of the trail of humble-self language in Scripture. I hope it will provide Christians with some fresh categories for thinking about humility and fresh avenues for pursuing humility in a humble way—and perhaps an unexpected vantage on the spiritual disciplines or "habits of grace" God gives us for the Christian life. I make no pretense in this book to capture a full theology of the virtue of humility, though our study will begin with a working definition in chapter 1. Specifically, I'm following the lead of the "humble-self" texts for what we might discover not as much about humility in general, though that's not unimportant, but specifically (and practically) about what it means to pursue humility, and especially to humble-self, when God is the one who initiates our humbling, not us.

Chapter 1

How Do I Humble Myself?

To the humble he gives favor.
Proverbs 3:34

Humility is beyond our grasp. It is not something we can achieve. We might consider it quintessentially American to think we could. *You can do it. Be proactive. Take the first step. Grab the bull by the horns and be humble.*

In other words, *humble yourself by your own bootstraps.*

But when we come to the Scriptures, we find ourselves in a different world. Genuine humility, as with genuine faith, is not self-help or a life hack, but a response to divine initiative and help. Yet before we assume too much, let's ask what *humility* is in biblical terms.

What Is Humility?

Fittingly, the first mention of humility in all the Bible comes in the escalating showdown between Egypt's Pharaoh and Israel's God, mediated through Moses.

Moses first dared to appear before Pharaoh in Exodus 5 and introduce him to "Yahweh," God's personal name revealed to him at the burning bush represented in our English translations as LORD in all caps. Moses speaks on Yahweh's behalf, "Let my people go." To which Pharaoh replies "Who is the LORD, that I should obey his voice and let Israel go? I do not know the LORD, and moreover, I will not let Israel go" (Exod. 5:2).

Mark that.

Pharaoh, swollen in his conception of self (pride), has miscalculated his status and abilities as a creature in relation to the Creator God. Through Moses, God speaks to Egypt's head and calls for him to *obey*. And Pharaoh refuses.

Exodus 10:3 then describes this as a call to humility. After seven plagues, on the cusp of an eighth,

God speaks to Pharaoh: "How long will you refuse to *humble yourself* before me?"

The piercing question, in the context of this extended power encounter, gives us this glimpse into the heart of humility: *humility acknowledges and obeys the one who is truly God.* Humility entails a right view of self, as created by and accountable to God—and this requires a right view of God, as Creator and as authoritative in relation to his creatures. Humility is not, then, preoccupied with oneself and one's own lowliness, but first mindful and conscious of God and his highness. Humility becomes conscious of self only with respect to God.

> Humility entails a right view of self, as created by and accountable to God.

Is God Humble?

Put another way, humility embraces the reality that *I am not God.* Pride led to humanity's fall when Adam and Eve desired to "be like God" (Gen. 3:5) contrary to his command. Humility would have trusted him and *obeyed* his command.

Humility, then, is a *creaturely virtue*. It is a posture of soul and body and life that acknowledges and embraces the goodness of God and the humanness of self, which means that "Is God humble?" is a tricky question. The answer is no, but not because God is the opposite of what we would consider humble. He is not arrogant or prideful. Rather, humility is a creaturely virtue, and he is God—Creator, not creature. The essence of humility, we might say with John Piper, is "to feel and think and say and act in a way that shows *I am not God*."[1] And genuine humility, as we will see, is not self-made or self-started, but a response to divine initiative and help. And we will see in chapter 8 what it means to be humble when God himself becomes man in the person of Christ.

---

[1] "Is God Humble?" Ask Pastor John podcast, April 17, 2020, available online at https://www.desiringgod.org/interviews/is -god-humble.

God Opposes the Proud

Make no mistake, we do have a part to play in humility. We are to *be humble*. It is to be truly *our humility*, though we might say *not our own*. Humility is not only an effect but a command. In particular, two apostles tell us directly to *humble ourselves*. And they do so in strikingly similar ways, adding the promise that God will exalt us on the other side:

> Humble yourselves before the Lord, and he will exalt you. (James 4:10)

> Humble yourselves . . . under the mighty hand of God so that at the proper time he may exalt you. (1 Pet. 5:6)

So far as we can tell, James and Peter haven't been inspired by each other on this point, but by the Old Testament. In the immediate context of instructing us to humble ourselves, both quote the Greek translation of Proverbs 3:34—"God opposes the proud but gives grace to the humble" (James 4:6; 1 Pet. 5:5). But before you run off to create your own program for self-humbling, at your initiative, with a list of your to-dos, let's linger here a few moments to consider the context in both passages.

Humbling from Within

We should note that both of these calls to self-humbling come *in response to trials*. James refers to quarrels and fights within the church:

> What causes *quarrels* and what causes
> *fights* among you? Is it not this, that
> your passions are at war within you?
> You desire and do not have, so you
> murder. You covet and cannot obtain,
> so *you fight and quarrel*. (James 4:1–2)

Conflict among those claiming the name of Christ humbles the church. It serves as a test of pride and humility. James not only reminds these quarreling Christians that they are "sinners" and "double-minded," but he also rehearses the divine promise of Proverbs 3:34. He charges the church to submit to

God, resist the devil, and draw near to God (James 4:7–8). In other words, "Humble yourselves before the Lord." The church is being humbled *from within*. Now, how will they respond to God's humbling purposes in this conflict? Will they humble themselves?

Humbling from Without

So also, in 1 Peter, the church is under external pressure. Society is mouthing insults and maligning these early Christians. They are beginning to suffer socially and emotionally, even if not yet physically. They are under growing threat and tempted to be anxious. And at this moment of humbling, Peter turns to Proverbs 3:34 and exhorts them, "Clothe yourselves, all of you, with humility toward one another" (1 Pet. 5:5).

Here the church's humbling is coming *from without*. Now, how will they respond to God's humbling purposes in these insults? Will they humble themselves? Will they bow up, reacting defensively with pride and self-exaltation, or will they bow down, humbling themselves before the gracious hand, rebuke, and perfect timing of their Lord?

Self-Humbling as Responsive

Over and over again in the Bible, self-humbling is not something we initiate but something we receive, even embrace, even welcome—when God does his humbling work—however direct or indirect his means. The invitation to *humble ourselves* does not come to us in a vacuum but through our first *being humbled*. First, God gets our attention with disruption, then invites us to welcome his mercy, however severe and painful.

Humility, like faith—and as a manifestation of faith—is not an achievement. Humility is not fundamentally a human initiative, but a proper, God-given response in us to God himself and his glory and his purposes in the world and in our lives.

We don't teach ourselves to be humble. There's no five-step plan for becoming more humble in the next week or month. Within measure, we might take certain steps, in faith, to cultivate a posture of humility in ourselves (more on those in chapters 3–7). But the main test (and opportunity) comes when we are confronted, unsettled, and accosted—in the moments when our semblances of control vanish and we're taken off guard by the hard edges of life in a fallen world—and the question comes to us: *How will you respond to these humbling circumstances? Will you humble yourself?*

Gladly Receive the Uncomfortable God

For Christians, self-humbling is mainly responsive. We don't initiate humility, and we don't get the credit for it. It's no less active and no less difficult, but it is responsive to who God is, what he has said to us in his Word, and what he is doing in the world, specifically as it comes to bear in all its inconvenience and pain and disappointment in our own lives. Self-humbling is, in essence, gladly receiving God's person, words, and acts when doing so is not easy or comfortable.

First come the disruptive words or circumstances, in God's hand and plan, that humble us—as it happened for King Hezekiah seven centuries before Christ. God healed him from his deathbed, and yet the king "did not make return according to the benefit done to him, for his heart was proud" (2 Chron. 32:25a). The king's enduring pride invited divine intervention, and necessitated its severity. In righteous wrath, though not without mercy, God took action against Hezekiah's pride. He humbled him. In whatever form it took, we're told that "wrath came upon him and Judah and Jerusalem" (v. 25b).

> Self-humbling is, in essence, gladly receiving God's person, words, and acts when doing so is not easy or comfortable.

Then comes the question that presses against our souls in our humbling providences, as it did for the king: Will I *receive* God's humbling or resist it? Will I try to explain it away or push back against it, or will it lead me to genuine repentance? If I do not *humble myself*, then further divine humbling will follow in time. God's initial humbling leads unavoidably to a further humbling. The question is whether it will be our self-humbling or further (and often more severe) humbling from him.

Hezekiah acknowledged the divine wrath as opposition to his own pride, and he "humbled himself for the pride of his heart, both he and the inhabitants of Jerusalem, so that the wrath of the LORD did not come upon them in the days of Hezekiah" (v. 26).

When God Humbles His People

To be sure, we are not left without some postures to cultivate and means to pursue. Daily humbling ourselves under the authority of God's Word, by obeying his words, and by coming desperately to him in prayer and in fasting—these all have their place in our overall response as creatures to our Creator. But first and foremost, we need to know humbling ourselves is a response to God.

God is the one who created our world from nothing by the power of his Word (Heb. 11:3). He is the one who formed the first man from the ground (Gen. 2:7) and the first woman from his side (Gen. 2:21–22). He is the one who chose to reveal himself to us, to speak words into our world through his prophets and apostles, to make known himself and his Son and his plan for our redemption. And he is the one who, through the gentleness and merciful severity of his providence, humbles his church again and again, from without and from within, and in his humbling brings us to the fork in the road: *Now, how will you respond to my humbling purposes in this trial? Will you humble yourself?*

This is the moment of choice we all have faced in our own stories, and we will face it again. Perhaps soon. Will you be ready? When the next humbling trial comes, will you bow up with pride, or bow down in humility before your Maker, Redeemer, and Friend? God has a particular promise for you in these moments. The God of all power will exalt the humble in his perfect timing.

> When the next humbling trial comes, will you bow up with pride, or bow down in humility before your Maker, Redeemer, and Friend?

Chapter 2

Humbled by the Hand of God

"Your heart was penitent,
and you humbled yourself before the Lord."
2 Kings 22:19

Humility is not self-taught, as we began to see in chapter 1. Try as we might, we don't just up and humble ourselves at our own time and pace.

Within measure, we can take certain modest steps to cultivate a posture of humility in ourselves, but the main test (and opportunity) comes when we are confronted, unsettled, and accosted, in the moments when our semblances of control vanish and we're taken off guard by the hard edges of life in a fallen world. In those moments, the question comes to us: *How will you respond to these humbling circumstances? Will you humble yourself?*

Humility Received, Not Achieved

God takes the initiative in producing humility in his people, as we have seen. Whether or not we will "humble ourselves" down here, then, comes in response to the humbling hand from above.

Alongside pondering the postures and means we can cultivate—as in daily humbling ourselves under the authority of God's Word, and humbling ourselves by obeying his words, and humbling ourselves by coming desperately to him in prayer, and humbling ourselves in fasting—we need to know that humbling ourselves is first and foremost a response to God, not our own design and plan.

When we find ourselves humbled—whether through God's Word, or becoming newly aware of some pattern of sin in us or some way we have not measured up, or some circumstances or event in life that lays us low—what might it mean to *humble ourselves*, looking with faith to the promise of God's lifting us up in his perfect timing?

Here in chapter 2, we will further explore the main message of this book by considering the self-humbling moments of three Old Testament kings—two Israelites, one Babylonian; two positive examples, one negative—and what we might glean for our time when it comes.

Receive the humbling of God, and repent.

God not only means for us to know ourselves to be sinners *generally* but also *specifically*. And in his goodness, he runs the world in such a way as to expose, in new ways, the specific sins of his people. In doing so, he calls us to admit particular times we have been on the wrong path and need to change course. The word for it is *repentance*.

Such repentance is a form of self-humbling, as demonstrated in the life of King Josiah.

When Hilkiah the high priest found the lost Book of the Law in the temple and brought it to the king, Josiah tore his clothes in distress as he became newly aware of how he and his people were out of step with God's directives (2 Kings 22:11). Josiah sent to inquire

of God, through the prophetess Huldah, who commended his self-humbling in the form of his repen-
tant heart and the acts that followed:

> "Thus says the LORD, the God of Israel:
> Regarding the words that you have
> heard, because *your heart was penitent,*
> *and you humbled yourself* before the
> LORD, when you heard how I spoke
> against this place and against its
> inhabitants, that they should become
> a desolation and a curse, and you have
> torn your clothes and wept before me,
> I also have heard you, declares the
> LORD." (2 Kings 22:18–19)

Josiah's repentance is recounted again in
2 Chronicles 34, with an emphasis on the king *hear-*
ing God's words and then appropriately responding
(called "self-humbling") with a tender heart and torn
garments: "because your heart was tender and you
humbled yourself before God when you *heard his*
words against this place and its inhabitants, and you

have humbled yourself before me and have torn your clothes and wept before me, I also have heard you, declares the LORD" (2 Chron. 34:27). As we'll see, this is just our first encounter with an arresting emphasis on self-humbling in 2 Chronicles.

Declare him to be right—always.

When life's circumstances and events conspire to lay us low, we may be tempted to doubt God's goodness and justice. The test of self-humbling in these moments, seen in King Rehoboam, is whether we arrogantly point the finger at God or humbly evaluate our own hearts and lives, declaring—for our own souls and for anyone else in earshot—that God is righteous.

Mark this word, which is increasingly countercultural today: it is never virtuous to doubt God's goodness and justice. We need to know, and be reminded, that *we have never been treated unfairly by God.* No creature ever has been mistreated by our righteous Creator. Never has he done you or anyone else wrong, however it was felt or perceived. He is not unjust and never will be unjust to you. And if we ever find ourselves suspecting him to be in the wrong, we can know that we ourselves are out of line, not him.[2]

It's one thing, however, to steady and correct our own souls. It's another to vocalize it.

Humility Lost and Found

Rehoboam, the son of Solomon, came to the throne in seeming strength and security, but he was off his spiritual guard and soon went soft. "When the rule of Rehoboam was established and he was strong, he abandoned the law of the LORD, and all Israel with him" (2 Chron. 12:1).

God's gracious humbling then came when Shishak king of Egypt "took the fortified cities of Judah and came as far as Jerusalem" (v. 4). This is no small, or distant, danger. It is humbling, to say the least, to have a foreign army march on your capital. The new-found threat to Jerusalem, and his own life, awakened

---

[2] I have reflected at greater length on this theme in an article titled "Never Blame God: How His Sovereignty Relates to Our Suffering," available online at https://www.desiringgod.org/articles/never-blame-god.

Rehoboam to his folly, and God sent the prophet Shemaiah to make God's purpose plain:

> Shemaiah the prophet came to Rehoboam and to the princes of Judah, who had gathered at Jerusalem because of Shishak, and said to them, "Thus says the LORD, 'You abandoned me, so I have abandoned you to the hand of Shishak.'" (2 Chron. 12:5)

In this instance, the king and his counselors "humbled themselves" by declaring God to be in the right and themselves to be in the wrong:

> Then the princes of Israel and the king humbled themselves and said, "The LORD is righteous." When the LORD saw that they humbled themselves, the word of the LORD came to Shemaiah: "They have humbled themselves. I will not destroy them, but I will grant them some deliverance, and my wrath shall not be poured out on Jerusalem

by the hand of Shishak." (2 Chron. 12:6–7)

Perhaps it bears asking today how many of us would have seen God's righteous hand in the invasion of a foreign army. Would we not seek to explain it mainly, if not exclusively, in human terms? Would we have the faith to recall that God stands directly or indirectly behind all that comes to pass? The question is not whether he is aware, and involved, and doing something for his glory and his people in the invasion of a foreign army or in anything that comes to pass. The question is not *whether* but *what*. He is at work. Precisely what he is doing is often hidden from our eyes, at least at first, but the eyes of faith are not content with mere human explanations and causes, real and significant as they are. In faith, we want to ask—not to make

> God stands directly or indirectly behind all that comes to pass.

pronouncements for others but for ourselves—*how might God be humbling me in this frowning providence?*

So, first, God acted to humble Rehoboam and his kingdom. Then, in his humbling, the king was presented with the moment of decision, as we are: *Will I humble myself before God, or resist in pride? Will I welcome his severe awakening, or kick against this kindness?*

Rehoboam humbled himself by declaring God to be in the right, and God had mercy on him: "when he humbled himself the wrath of the LORD turned from him, so as not to make a complete destruction" (2 Chron. 12:12).

Learn from the humbling of others.

Finally, one other regal example is instructive for us who desire to be more humble and yet admit our inability to up and do it for ourselves. This time the example is negative.

In the case of Belshazzar, king of Babylon, the humbling he should have learned from was not his own but that of his (grand)father, Nebuchadnezzar. Carried away at a party, and swollen with pride, Belshazzar brought out to use for debauchery "the vessels of gold and of silver that Nebuchadnezzar

his father had taken out of the temple in Jerusalem"
(Dan. 5:2).

When the fingers of a human hand appeared
and wrote on the wall, and the king himself saw
the hand as it wrote, his color changed with alarm.
His own magi could not interpret the words, but
the queen remembered Daniel, and he was summoned to the king's aid. Before giving his interpreta-
tion, Daniel reminded Belshazzar of his grandfather,
whom God humbled, and what it should have meant
to Belshazzar:

> "When his [Nebuchadnezzar's] heart
> was lifted up and his spirit was hard-
> ened so that he dealt proudly, he was
> brought down from his kingly throne,
> and his glory was taken from him. He
> was driven from among the children
> of mankind, and his mind was made
> like that of a beast, and his dwelling
> was with the wild donkeys. He was
> fed grass like an ox, and his body was
> wet with the dew of heaven, until he

knew that the Most High God rules the kingdom of mankind and sets over it whom he will. And you his son, Belshazzar, have not humbled your heart, *though you knew all this*, but you have lifted up yourself against the Lord of heaven." (Dan. 5:20–23)

God's humbling of Nebuchadnezzar was a lesson not only for him, but also for his kingdom and for his progeny—and not just his contemporaries but even his grandsons. But this grandson didn't take notice, and it was too late. "That very night Belshazzar the Chaldean king was killed" (Dan. 5:30).

Learning from God's humbling of others is vital for each of us, and not just in our own day but from the generations before us. God not only means to humble us all individually—and he has his countless ways of doing so in the tough mercies of his providence—but he also means for us to humble ourselves in response to seeing others humbled, both around us and before us. Wisdom not only humbles herself in response to her own humbling, but also in response to the humbling of others.

God is the one who does the humbling, and he will get the glory for it. In this is humility—not that we have humbled our-selves, but that God, in his mercy, took action to humble us first. Yet, he invites us to welcome his work and participate in the process through the self-humbling of repent-ing, declaring him righteous, and learning from the humbling of others.

> In this is humility—not that we have humbled ourselves, but that God, in his mercy, took action to humble us first.

Chapter 3

Word: Humility Begins with Hearing

"Your heart was tender and you
humbled yourself before God
when you heard his words."
2 Chronicles 34:27

Humility, as we've seen, is not the product of self-help. Any do-it-yourself "humility," rooted in our own ingenuity, is but pride masquerading as its enemy. Genuine humility is the work and initiative of God.

Yet that does not mean that we human creatures have no part to play. Our humbling, at God's lead, involves our minds and hearts and wills and behaviors. And while there is no simple program for making ourselves truly humble, God has given us examples to follow, as we saw in chapter 2. He has also given us some practices and patterns to cultivate and sustain.

Note well that developing habits and rhythms of life that ready us to receive God's initiative is not the same as, but a far cry from, setting out on our initiative to develop humility. The "habits of grace" that God's Word commends for our preparation for self-humbling are not directions for securing humility. Habits that cultivate in us sensitivity to God's grace and initiative are not a "get it done" approach to Christian humility. Nor is humility something we only wait on, to be given us passively.

Humility is not our doing without God's initiative and empowering, and it's not something he acts exclusively to do for us, which we receive passively. In this chapter, we will begin to see how God's initiative and ongoing grace in the Christian life lead us to patterns and habits that prepare us to respond with humility and humble ourselves, when his humbling hand falls in his timing.

Perhaps the single most important habit we can develop, or at least the first and primary means God uses, is the daily and weekly welcoming of his Word in the Scriptures.

Glad Reverence and Submission

Every new morning presents a fresh opportunity to bend our hearts toward humility—or to re-calcify them in our native pride.

Each rising sun brings with it the question, Will you try to handle this day on your own, or reconsecrate yourself with a renewed declaration of dependence? And in particular, Will you begin this day with the sound of God's voice, the whispers of your own, or the words of someone else? Some voice will be the first you hear—and the first you heed for the day's direction. Will it be yours? Will it be the opinions and demands of fellow humans? Will it be the world's voice through various media—the voices of political polemics on news media, the voices of comparison and complaint on social media, the voices of self-help in popular podcasts? Or will it be the only words that truly give life?[3]

Welcoming God's voice, or rejecting it, not only happens at the top of every day, but also the top of every week. Each Lord's Day corporate gathering of the church offers a new opportunity to bow gladly beneath the hearing and proclamation of God's Word, or bow up with the pride of our own ideas. How we hear each Scripture read, and sermon preached, conditions our souls, for better or worse, toward humility or self-confidence.

> Will you begin this day with the sound of God's voice, the whispers of your own, or the words of someone else?

Whether a morning reading, or a Sunday sermon, or a verse spoken and applied by a friend, we must

---

[3] I have written more about making God's voice the first you hear each morning in an article called "Seize the Morning," available online at https://www.desiringgod.org/articles/seize -the-morning.

decide how we will respond to God's Word. What will be our reflex to divine initiative when we hear the voice of God in Scripture? What instinctive response will we develop words from God that confront our sin and land on us as unpleasant, even painful? Will we respond with reverence and glad-hearted submission? Will we make a habit of welcoming God's Word, or subtly resisting it?

How to Hear from God

How we respond to the words of God can reveal how our journey toward humility is progressing. God himself makes the point with unusual clarity in the lives of two righteous kings some centuries before Christ.

First, when Hezekiah came to the throne—on the heels of King Ahaz, who "did not do what was right in the eyes of the LORD" (2 Chron. 28:1)—Hezekiah led the cleansing of the temple and rededicating of the priests. Once the temple was "made ready and consecrated" (2 Chron. 29:19), he decreed "a proclamation throughout all Israel, from Beersheba to Dan, that the people should come and keep the Passover to the LORD, the God of Israel, at Jerusalem, for they had not kept it *as often as prescribed*" (2 Chron. 30:5–6). Prescribed by whom? By God himself, in his Word.

As much as this may have looked like Hezekiah's idea, he was not the one acting first. God had spoken first. Centuries before. And tragically, his people had not done what God had said. But now Hezekiah was listening. He welcomed God's Word, uncomfortable as it was, and summoned his people to join him anew. And how the people would respond to the proclamation—whether in pride or self-humbling—wouldn't owe ultimately to Hezekiah but to the Word of God:

> The couriers went from city to city through the country of Ephraim and Manasseh, and as far as Zebulun, but they laughed them to scorn and mocked them. However, some men of Asher, of Manasseh, and of Zebulun *humbled themselves* and came to Jerusalem. The hand of God was

also on Judah to give them one heart
to do what the king and the princes
commanded *by the word of the* LORD.
(2 Chron. 30:10–12)

The prideful rejected God's Word and mocked the
king's messengers—just as many do today when confronted by divine words
from centuries ago. But
others welcomed God's
Word and humbled them-
selves. The same is still
true: the proud resist
what God has com-
manded, while the hum-
ble cherish and gladly
submit to his words.

> The proud resist
> what God has
> commanded, while
> the humble cherish
> and gladly submit
> to his words.

When You Hear His Words

Less than a century later, the words of God played
the decisive role in the self-humbling of King Josiah
and his people, as we saw in chapter 1. Hilkiah the

high priest found "the Book of the Law of the LORD given through Moses" (2 Chron. 34:14) and sent it to the king. Then came the moment of decision: How would Josiah respond? Would he welcome God's Word or reject it?

When Josiah heard what God had said, he humbled himself (2 Chron. 34:19). He sent for counsel to the prophetess Huldah, who responded,

> "Thus says the LORD, the God of Israel: Regarding the words that you have heard, because your heart was tender and *you humbled yourself before God when you heard his words* against this place and its inhabitants, and *you have humbled yourself before me* and have torn your clothes and wept before me, I also have heard you, declares the LORD." (2 Chron. 34:26–27)

God took action *through his words* to humble the king and the nation. These were not new words, but words God had given his people long ago—just as we too hold his words in our hands today. As we seek to humble ourselves before him, we are not left waiting for some fresh word from heaven, but invited to press our ears and hearts to the words we already have in Scripture.

As the old hymn "How Firm a Foundation" asks, "What more can he say than to you he has said?" No Christian should complain of any famine of God's Word. We have an oasis, a veritable endless supply of life-giving water, in our access to the Bible.

How Not to Hear God

However, while Hezekiah and Josiah serve as good examples of how to welcome God's words, King Zedekiah, tragically not many years after Josiah, models the horrors of rejecting the divine voice. Again, 2 Chronicles tells the story:

> Zedekiah was twenty-one years old when he began to reign, and he reigned eleven years in Jerusalem. He did what was evil in the sight of the

Lord his God. *He did not humble himself* before Jeremiah the prophet, who spoke from the mouth of the Lord. (2 Chron. 36:11–12)

To reject Jeremiah, who spoke as a prophet on God's behalf, was to reject God himself. Jeremiah laments the calamity of a prideful people who do "not listen or incline their ear" (Jer. 44:5) to God's word:

"They have not humbled themselves even to this day, nor have they feared, nor walked in my law and my statutes that I set before you and before your fathers." (Jer. 44:10)

To ignore the voice of God in his Word is to ignore God himself.

We see this play out in the life of Zedekiah, who did not welcome God's words. To ignore the voice of God in his Word is to ignore God himself. And could anything be more serious, dangerous, and tragic than this?

How to Welcome the Words of God

If we are ready to gladly and reverently submit to whatever God says, can we say anything else about *how* we are to receive his Word? Two further examples from Scripture provide at least two specific pursuits to keep in mind as we make a daily and weekly habit of welcoming God's words.

Work to Understand What God Says

I say "work" rather than simply "seek" because understanding an author, on his terms, takes energy and effort. Active reading is a form of work. Rewarding work. Work that is manifestly worth it. Active reading takes more time, more effort, and more attention (and often a pencil). It means moving at the pace of the text, rather than the pace of modern society. It means pausing and going back to reread a sentence you didn't quite understand. Sometimes going back and rereading whole paragraphs, even chapters.

One model here is that exemplary exile in Babylon, Daniel. He set his heart to understand God's word through the writings of Jeremiah (Dan. 9:2–3), and when an angel visited him, Daniel was commended for humbly seeking to understand God on God's terms:

> "Fear not, Daniel, for from the first day that *you set your heart to understand and humbled yourself before your God,* your words have been heard, and I have come because of your words." (Dan. 10:12)

Daniel did not twist God's words to make them seem convenient and comfortable at the time. Rather, he humbled himself by setting his heart *to understand.*

It's an often overlooked "be like Daniel" lesson for today. God means for us to gladly receive his word—what he really says, with all the edges and inconveniences.

We welcome God's words by cultivating the mentality that divine truths, if we are really listening, don't typically go down easily for fallen, finite humans. We should be more surprised when extended portions of Scripture land on us without any measure of discomfort, than when we are, in some way, unsettled.

Seek to Obey with His Help

Yet one more thing we can say about humbling ourselves through welcoming God's words is *obedience*. Humble understanding is the root. Humble obedience is the fruit. None other than Pharaoh is our (negative) example here, as we saw in chapter 1. After the seventh plague, Moses went to him and said,

> "Thus says the LORD, the God of the Hebrews, 'How long will you *refuse to humble yourself* before me? Let my people go, that they may serve me.'" (Exod. 10:3)

God's Word had come through Moses to Pharaoh, and the least we can say is that he did not welcome it. He heard it. He understood it adequately enough. But he did not obey it—not just initially, but after seven plagues, and demonstration after demonstration of

God's power. Pharaoh's heart was hard with the recalcitrance of pride, and he refused to obey.

Centuries later, James would exhort his readers to "receive with meekness the implanted word" (James 1:21), and then add, "But be doers of the word, and not hearers only, deceiving yourselves" (James 1:22). Welcoming God's words all the way down means obeying them. Not just hearing. And not just understanding. God wants the kind of hearing and understanding that leads to action in his creatures. Obedience. Change of heart. New habits of life. New patterns. New desperate pleas for everyday help from the Holy Spirit.

Fork in the Word

Do you want to be ready when God's humbling hand seemingly intrudes into your life? Put yourself under his Word daily in Bible intake and weekly under faithful Bible preaching in the life of your local church.

The very parting of the ways, far upstream, between those who humble themselves before God and those who resist his will and ways, goes back to this simple fork: Will we develop regular habits of welcoming his words—in all their comfort and discomfort, all their sweetness and inconvenience, all their warmth and edges? Will we work to understand and seek to obey the words of our God?[4]

---

[4] I have attempted to discuss these habits in practical detail in the article "How to Read the Bible Better," available online at https://www.desiringgod.org/articles/how-to-read-the-bible -better, and at greater length still in *Habits of Grace: Enjoying Jesus through the Spiritual Disciplines* (Crossway, 2016).

Chapter 4

Prayer: Sound of the Humbled

"If my people . . .
humble themselves, and pray . . ."
2 Chronicles 7:14

Self-humbling is a grace beyond our own grasp. It's a blessing we await, not achieve. As we have seen, God is the one who takes the first and decisive action in mercifully humbling his people. Yet he has not left us only to wait, in silence and without action. In fact, he wants to hear our voice. He invites us to have his ear.

Various habits of life can bend our souls toward humility and form instincts that shape us to gladly receive God's severe mercies when they come. One, as we saw in chapter 3, is welcoming God's Word in Bible reading and meditation, and sitting attentively under faithful preaching and teaching.

However, the cycle of preparation for self-humbling lies incomplete without the counterpart to welcoming his voice—namely, letting our own be heard, by appealing to him in prayer.

Own Your Desperation

In one sense, we are accenting here the importance of prayer in all its many shades and modes—from adoration of God in his holiness, to confession of sin, to expression of gratitude, to petitioning him for daily needs, to interceding for others. All prayer both expresses and cultivates in us a sense of dependence on God; however, when we know ourselves especially desperate, and appeal to God for rescue in the face of some looming threat, we experience an intensity that the Scriptures connect to self-humbling.

To appeal to God for rescue moves us beyond the casual requests that pour forth from our casual lives. It's one thing to put together a wish list; it's quite another to beg for deliverance from life-threatening peril. We most humble ourselves in prayer when we appeal to God for what is plainly beyond our ability to produce. We feel stuck or cornered. We are desperate. We have come to the end of ourselves and our resourcefulness. And in our appeal to him is a more pronounced acknowledgment of his highness and our lowness, his strength and our weakness, his omnipotent ability and our human inability, his holiness and our humility.

> We most humble ourselves in prayer when we appeal to God for what is plainly beyond our ability to produce.

If My People

Already we have seen more self-humbling texts from 2 Chronicles. The theme is more conspicuous and extended here than anywhere else in Scripture. This was the season of Israel's great humbling. Often

God humbled his people quite apart from their welcoming it. For instance, under Ahaz, "the LORD humbled Judah because of Ahaz king of Israel, for he had made Judah act sinfully and had been very unfaithful to the LORD" (2 Chron. 28:19).

However, at key junctures, the people, led by a righteous king, humbled themselves by seeing and acknowledging God's humbling work. Once God had acted to humble them, then the question came: *Would they receive his humbling?* Would they humble themselves? Or would they kick and squirm? Would they fight back against his humbling hand, or write it off as random, unfortunate circumstance? Or would they see and acknowledge God at work in it and *kiss the wave*, as many have said, that had thrown them against the Rock of Ages?

From the height of the kingdom under Solomon, to the utter depths of decimation under Babylon, God's humbling hand was received, notably at points, with self-humbling—by Rehoboam (2 Chron. 12:6–7, 12), by Hezekiah (2 Chron. 28:19; 30:11; 32:26), and by Josiah (2 Chron. 34:27). At other times, his humbling was rejected, demonstrated perhaps most starkly in Zedekiah who "did not humble himself before Jeremiah the prophet, who spoke from the mouth of the LORD" (2 Chron. 36:12).

Humble Yourself and Pray

Likely the most often-quoted text today on self-humbling, though, is the first mention of this theme in 2 Chronicles. After Solomon had completed the temple and offered his great dedicatory prayer, God appeared to him and said, "I have heard your prayer and have chosen this place for myself as a house of sacrifice" (2 Chron. 7:12).

Then come the words many of us have heard time and again (even if the initial *when* clause is omitted):

> "When I shut up the heavens so that there is no rain, or command the locust to devour the land, or send pestilence among my people, if my people who are called by my name *humble themselves, and pray* and seek my face and turn from their wicked ways,

then I will hear from heaven and will
forgive their sin and heal their land."
(2 Chron. 7:13–14)

Not *if* there is no rain someday, but *when*. And *when*
God sends locusts and pestilence. Not *if* he sends
pandemics, but *when*.

The days of humbling will come. The nation
will decline in time; it's in the plan. God will act,
in response to their sin,
with drought and fam-
ine and disease, to make
the people freshly des-
perate. And in those
times, self-humbling will
mean *prayer*—his people
appealing to him for help.
*Humble yourselves and pray
and seek my face and turn
from your wicked ways.*

In such moments,
self-humbling requires
turning from the path of

> Self-humbling
> requires turning
> from the path of
> pride, spiritual
> apathy, and self-
> reliance that
> is leading to
> destruction, and
> turning to the face
> of God in prayer.

pride, spiritual apathy, and self-reliance that is leading to destruction, and turning to the face of God in
prayer. And those who are most ready to hit their
knees in desperate times will be those who have
learned the habit of bowing even in the best of times.

When Manasseh Refused to Pray

King Manasseh's story is an extraordinary glimpse
into the depths of God's grace and the role of prayer in
self-humbling. His life reminds us that the narrowness
of the path of humility is due to the hardness of human
hearts, not any lack in the breadth of God's mercy.

Overall, Manasseh, son of Hezekiah, is remembered as a wicked king (2 Kings 21:2; 2 Chron. 33:2).
His sin was so grave that God promised,

> "Because Manasseh king of Judah has
> committed these abominations and
> has done things more evil than all that
> the Amorites did, who were before him,
> and has made Judah also to sin with
> his idols, therefore thus says the LORD,

> the God of Israel: Behold, I am bringing
> upon Jerusalem and Judah such disas-
> ter that the ears of everyone who hears
> of it will tingle." (2 Kings 21:11–12)

Not just difficulty but disaster—ear-tingling disaster. Every ounce of it deserved, due to the unusual depravity of Manasseh (more evil than all the Amorites, known for their evil). Even once the good king Josiah had come to the throne and implemented extensive reforms, the depths of national depravity under Manasseh could not be overcome, however much Josiah tried (2 Kings 23:26). And when Babylon came to destroy Jerusalem, God tied it explicitly to Manasseh: "Surely this came upon Judah at the command of the LORD, to remove them out of his sight, *for the sins of Manasseh*, according to all that he had done" (2 Kings 24:3).

When Manasseh Bowed to Pray

But oh, the mercy of God! Even for one so wicked as Manasseh, one who had so plainly "led Judah and the inhabitants of Jerusalem astray" (2 Chron. 33:9). When God "brought upon [his people] the commanders of the army of the king of Assyria, who captured Manasseh with hooks and bound him with chains of bronze and brought him to Babylon" (v. 11), Manasseh, in his desperation, turned to God in prayer:

> When he was in distress, he entreated the favor of the LORD his God and *humbled himself greatly* before the God of his fathers. *He prayed to him, and God was moved by his entreaty and heard his plea* and brought him again to Jerusalem into his kingdom. Then Manasseh knew that the LORD was God. (2 Chron. 33:12–13)

This ungodly king, depraved as he had been, appealed to God in desperation—in the self-humbling act of prayer. At long last, he had come to the end of himself and his own resources and power. Now he was willing to admit he needed God's rescue, at least for the moment, and he made his plea in desperation.

And even for such a wicked man, the king whose evil in the history of God's people may have been unsurpassed, God opened his ear. God stood ready to be "moved by his entreaty"—even when he knew it would be short-lived.

For those of us in Christ, we have all the more reason, in our desperation, to hit our knees and plead for help in the wideness of God's mercy. If God heard Manasseh, then how much more will he hear our self-humbling cries in Christ and be moved to send his rescue in his perfect way and time? How much more for those of us who now have the Great High Priest, able to sympathize with our weakness, bidding us "with confidence draw near to the throne of grace, that we may receive mercy and find grace to help in time of need" (Heb. 4:16)?

Mark the Trail to Heaven

Prayer is a sacred act for humbled humans. In prayer, we turn from being disillusioned with our own resources and strength. And if we are to learn well from Manasseh's self-humbling (as his son did not—2 Chronicles 33:23), we will not wait until we are in dire straits to turn Godward and appeal for divine help. We will make it a pattern now, threaded into the very fabric of our days and weeks, mornings and midday and evenings, alone and together, scheduled and spontaneous.

Humility in the worst of times grows out of habits of prayerful desperation in the best of times. For those of us who are under the delusion that we are strong, prayer makes little sense, especially as a pattern of life. But when we freshly realize our fragileness and weakness, we find that the New Testament's emphasis on unceasing prayer (1 Thess. 5:17) is not a burden but an unparalleled offer.

> For those of us who are under the delusion that we are strong, prayer makes little sense, especially as a pattern of life.

Because we are so needy, what grace to learn that we can "be constant in prayer" (Rom. 12:12). Such a charge lands on the desperate as an opportunity, not an obligation. How can we not make good on such access? That God does not tire of our pleas or close his ears to us, but we can "continue steadfastly in prayer" (Col. 4:2). That we need not "be anxious about anything, but in everything by prayer and supplication with thanksgiving let [our] requests be made known to God" (Phil. 4:6).

Not only do we have Christ interceding for us, but also his Spirit, who "helps us in our weakness. For we do not know what to pray for as we ought, but the Spirit himself intercedes for us with groanings too deep for words" (Rom. 8:26). When we know our desperation, and the nearness of our Lord and his Helper, how can we not be among those who delight to be "praying at all times in the Spirit, with all prayer and supplication" (Eph. 6:18)?

Don't wait till God's humbling hand descends. Walk the path today, on your knees. Mark now the trail to heaven. Learn to look Godward as a reflex, long before your great humblings come. And when they do, under God, you'll be far more ready.

Chapter 5

Fellowship: You Are Not That Special

"Rejoice that your names are written in heaven."
Luke 10:20

I had a professor in seminary who had a knack for humbling first-year students. He enjoyed demonstrating, to great extent, that they weren't special, despite what their Sunday school teachers and home churches had made them think. In fact, this professor was so effective at humbling new seminarians, he developed a bit of a reputation for it.

He was provocative and polarizing. He had his detractors around campus and beyond. To some, he seemed cocky and headstrong. But others loved him dearly. *Dearly*. Not mainly because he could walk the line between arrogance and purposeful provocation, but because they themselves had been wonderfully awakened.

First, they had been humbled by his jabs, and it hurt. It was disorienting. But as much as it smarted at first, some students came to humble themselves and receive the uncomfortable truths. The professor's shocking words proved to be the wounds of a friend. He was right. They weren't that special—not in the ways that many seminary students (and humans) tend to think of themselves.

You Are (Not) Special

For many of us, one of the earliest messages we heard, the constant refrain of children's books, the chorus of our parents (and especially grandparents), and likely even the message we heard in Sunday school, was essentially *you are special*.

There's an element of truth in it, of course. You are indeed special—as a creature of God almighty, and especially as redeemed in his Son—in ways that redound to the glory of God. In relation to nature and the animal kingdom, God made our human race special, *in his own image*. Just a little poking around in recent neurological studies will leave most of us in awe of humanity.

As much as some anthropologists may resist the ancient Judeo-Christian maxim of humanity as "the crown of creation," their research can't help but bear out the reality. Humans are indeed set apart. And that's just with respect to creation.

As for redemption, even the heavenly beings marvel at the grace we've received in Christ, "things into which angels long to look" (1 Pet. 1:12). In Christ, no doubt, you are *special* to God, defined in a certain way—through being chosen before the foundation of the world and then particularly redeemed by the sacrifice of Christ two millennia before you were born. We might even say three times special by the regenerating work of the Holy Spirit.

Jesus died for his friends (John 15:13), his sheep (John 10:14–15), his bride (Eph. 5:25). He loved the church with his special love and gave himself up for her. "God, being rich in mercy, because of the *great love* with which he loved us, even when we were dead in our trespasses, made us alive together with Christ" (Eph. 2:4–5). In Christ, you are not just loved, but greatly so.

And on the human level, children are indeed special to their parents and grandparents. Let's grant that. It's in God's good design.

Also, it's worth acknowledging that a group of peculiarly self-doubting humans and saints have a difficult time believing they are special in the ways we've just rehearsed. Perhaps they've been so beaten down by life in this world—or maybe simply found low self-esteem to be a convenient excuse for coddling sin. To be human, and alive, is amazing. To be called a child of the living God by being joined to his Son, by faith, is scandalously glorious. Chosen *by God* before you even did anything good or bad! What wondrous love is this?

But oh, how prone we can be, like first-year seminarians, to let the thought of specialness go to our heads—to bend the truth of our God-glorifying specialness into avenues that serve the flesh rather the Spirit.

Not That Special

When sinners contemplate their own specialness, we don't typically think about our relation to animals or angels, or what it means to be in Christ, or our particular specialness to family and friends. Rather, we often think we're special compared to others—because of our qualities. Our impressive abilities. Our timeless achievements. Our clever angles. Bells that ring to our own glory. Like the young Tom Riddle, who would become the horrible Lord

> We often think we're special compared to others.

Voldemort, whispered to his own quivering fingers, "I knew I was special." Later Dumbledore would tell Harry Potter, "Yes, Riddle was perfectly ready to believe that he was—to use his word—*special*."[5]

We need to hear a clear, and sometimes forceful, voice say, in love, *You are not that special.*

---

[5] J. K. Rowling, *Harry Potter and the Half-Blood Prince* (Arthur A. Levin Books, 2005), 225–26.

You are not an exception to the basic laws and ordinances of human society, and as a Christian, you are not an exception to the ordinary means and patterns of the Christian life. You are not a cut above the rank-and-file in the world, and especially in the church. You are not exceptional in the ways you might like to tell yourself in the silence of your own head.

You are not special in the sense that ordinary, everyday, normal Christianity is no longer essential to you because of your qualities. *You are not that special.* You don't have a special path to heaven or a special route through the toils and snares of this world.

Just consider Jesus. He is indeed the Father's *special* Son. If anyone could plead special privilege, it would be the divine Son. And yet! He did not cling to his equality with God as a self-serving privilege or ask to be excused from the sweat and blood of the mission. He did not request a pass from poverty, suffering, or even torture. He became "obedient to the point of death, even death on a cross" (Phil. 2:8).

We'll linger here together, on the self-humbling of Christ, when we come to the end of our study. There is so much to marvel at in the self-humbling of Christ.

Do we claim to be his disciples, yet presume ourselves greater than our Master?

Inconvenient Specialness

How might we discern whether we are appropriating specialness in the right ways? One test would be whether we tell ourselves we're special in ways that are easy and convenient for the flesh, in ways that serve our sin. Do I presume I'll get my way because I'm special? Should others follow my lead, without my earning their trust, because I'm special?

Another way at it might be this: Do I love the specialness of humanity, and being Christ's, only when it applies to me, but not when it applies to those I find most difficult to endure?

This gets at what may be one of the greatest indicators of humility in our generation: how we view the local church. Not just the big, universal, capital-C Church—the one that is often much easier to love. But *your* church. The local church where God has placed you. The people God has picked to appear, and reappear, and reappear again, in your real-life story. Those faces and flaws. That church. With all the warts and frustrations and inconveniences you're increasingly aware of.

When you ponder the flesh-and-blood Christians you know, and worship with weekly, and share the Table with, do you think of yourself as special *in distinction* to them? Or are you special *with* them?

Really Belong to His Body

Local churches can be wonderfully humbling collectives. And one of the chief ways God roughs up our souls, and keeps them in shape, and prepares them to welcome his humbling hand when it descends—and often brings the very conflicts that are his humbling work—is through our

> Local churches can be wonderfully humbling collectives.

belonging to a particular, imperfect local body of fellow believers.

Really belong. Really join. Make the objective commitment of church membership. Whether your church calls it "membership," "partnership," or something else, the New Testament assumes some form of committed, accountable belonging as a reality for every true follower of Jesus. Each Christian has a definite place of local belonging. To be baptized is to become part of a particular local body. And formally *joining*—not just floating in and out, but making yourself accountable to a local church—not only serves the good of others, the pastors, and even unbelievers, but profoundly serves your own joy and perseverance and humbling.[6]

Church membership humbles us by committing us to an objective, real-life, relational community in which we share the joys and pains of life together in Christ. In submitting ourselves *to the church's elders,* we are humbled under faithful teaching from God's

---

[6] For more on church membership, and six reasons to put down roots, see "Why Join a Church," available online at https://www.desiringgod.org/articles/why-join-a-church.

Word and wise application to church life through their oversight. And in the local church, we submit *to each other,* as fellow members, both in the truth we speak into each other's lives, as well as in our knowing we are not our own but represent others. Our local church is our in-the-flesh reminder that in all we do, we bear the name of our Lord. Our words and conduct in the world reflect our God and his people.

Church membership also subjects us to sometimes uncomfortable, and regularly precious, interactions with people with whom we seem to have little in common, except for Christ. More than ever, our modern lives are disconnected from neighbors and extended family. We pick our friends, and they're often eerily like us. But not typically in the church. A glory of our Savior is that he often draws together, in his diverse excellencies, those who have very little common ground other than him. Both the hardest and best interactions and relationships of our lives come in local churches where we are committed to each other, and stay with it when it's uncomfortable, and don't flee at the first sign of conflict.

Among countless blessings, one gift that the messy, often difficult life of the local church offers us, if we will let it, is the regular reminder that we're not that special, not in the twisted ways we might like to tell ourselves. We are indeed special to God *with* these people—as lowly and unimpressive as they may be— but not *in comparison with* them.

And what the down-to-earth life of the local church reminds us is how good it can be to be normal, and to remember, for our good, that no Christian is exempt from normal Christianity: from repentance, from trust in Christ alone for forgiveness, from the moment-by-moment help of his Spirit, from saturating our lives in the Word of God, from daily availing ourselves of his ear in prayer, and from genuinely belonging to his body in a local church.

Good to Be Normal

Brothers and sisters, let's rehearse for ourselves, as much as we need it, that we are indeed special, and at the same time not *that* special, not in ways convenient to our flesh.

71

And let's celebrate that together with Jesus' church, we are indeed special. You are special—*you plural.*

Jesus loved the church and gave himself up for her. He laid down his life for his sheep. Through faith in Jesus, we are joined to him, and not alone. In him we also are joined to his people, his bride, his flock, his friends. He has loved *us* with his special, electing, and effective love.

We glory in this specialness, and die to sin's temptation to think of ourselves as special in ways that swell our hearts with conceit. We submit to belonging, truly belonging, to the fellowship of the church.

Chapter 6

Humble Yourself and Fast

I wept and humbled my soul with fasting.
Psalm 69:10

A*m I humble?*

It's a tough question to answer. For one thing, humble people don't spend a lot of time thinking about themselves, especially their own humility. But it may be a constructive question to ask on occasion. And what if you started that next self-evaluation by asking, "When's the last time I fasted?"

Fasting, biblically speaking, is an act of self-humbling. Prayer, we might say, is the quintessential act of self-humbling, as we confess to God some inability on our part, and attribute decisive power to him, and plead for his help. And particular intensity in prayer, born in days of unusual desperation, can be especially self-humbling, as we saw in chapter 4. These kinds of prayers in Scripture are often accompanied with fasting.

> Fasting can be an indicator of genuine humility.

Without being an exact measuring stick, fasting can be an indicator of genuine humility. Whether you're considering fasting afresh, or for the first time, as an act of self-humbling, it may be valuable to rehearse four often overlooked Old Testament passages that explicitly connect fasting with self-humbling.

None So Evil

The first comes in a most surprising place, in the life of one of Israel's all-time worst figures: Ahab, whose very name has become proverbial for evil.

Few leaders in the history of Israel descended to such depths of depravity.

In 1 Kings 21, King Ahab desires to acquire the vineyard of a man named Naboth, because it is near to the palace. When Naboth refuses to sell, Ahab's wicked wife, Jezebel, whose name has become proverbial in its own right (Rev. 2:20) as one who incited her husband to sin (1 Kings 21:25), arranges to have Naboth falsely accused and stoned. Once he is dead, Ahab seizes his vineyard.

God then speaks to Ahab through the king's nemesis, the prophet Elijah:

> "Thus says the LORD, 'Have you killed and also taken possession? . . . Behold, I will bring disaster upon you. I will utterly burn you up, and will cut off from Ahab every male, bond or free, in Israel.'" (1 Kings 21:19, 21)

The narrator reminds us, while we wait for Ahab's response, "There was none who sold himself to do what was evil in the sight of the LORD like Ahab" (1 Kings 21:25). Surely, such an evil king, with such a record of recalcitrance, will write off this judgment. He might even spit in the prophet's face, or attempt to have him killed.

None So Merciful

Instead, the almost imponderable happens. "When Ahab heard those words [from Elijah], he tore his clothes and put sackcloth on his flesh and fasted and lay in sackcloth and went about dejectedly" (1 Kings 21:27). Ahab humbled himself and fasted before God. And as unlikely as this wicked king's self-humbling might have been, God's response is all the more surprising.

God speaks to Elijah again,

> "Have you seen how Ahab has *humbled himself* before me? Because he has *humbled himself* before me, I will not bring the disaster in his days; but in his son's days I will bring the disaster upon his house." (1 Kings 21:29)

It's a measured word, for sure, but a startling mercy nonetheless. Disaster is not averted for the dynasty, but it is for Ahab. This is not unlike God's staggering mercy we saw in chapter 4 on wicked king Manasseh. How ready is our God to show mercy, even for one almost peerless in evil? God looked on Ahab's humbling himself, expressed through fasting, and God put the disaster on hold.

Fasting as Self-Humbling

Fasting—not only for Ahab, but throughout Scripture—is temporarily abstaining from food for a spiritual purpose. One might abstain from other practices that are otherwise good, but fasting *from food* is especially fitting. Food is vital for life, and yet God has equipped humans with the ability (unpleasant as it may be) to go without food for days on end, even as long as three weeks. (By contrast, we can go without breathing only for a few minutes, and without water only a few days.)

Just as God designed our bodies for food, he also designed them for fasting. But fasting, as a spiritual discipline, is not the normal state. It is a temporary and occasional measure for seeking God in some special way. Fasting declares, "God, you are even more important than something so basic as daily bread—which I'm going without in view of this special need for more of you."

> Fasting declares, "God, you are even more important than something so basic as daily bread."

Fasting is an act of self-humbling by declaring our need to God, and by allowing ourselves to see afresh how weak we really are, as we experience the anxiety and irritability that come with an empty stomach.

Responsive Fasting

Perhaps Christians today typically think of fasting (if we think of it at all) as a scheduled practice. Under the terms of the old covenant, God's people observed scheduled fasts. So also, some today (may their number increase!) observe weekly or monthly fasts, whether individually or corporately.

But Ahab's surprising act of self-humbling marks another important way of thinking about fasting, one that often goes overlooked: fasting *as a response* when God humbles us. Ahab didn't have this fast on his calendar. It wasn't his plan or initiative. God broke in unbidden and interrupted Ahab's pattern of sin. God's prophet confronted him, exposed his sin, and announced judgment. First, God humbled Ahab. Then, the king responded by fasting.

At least in this moment, Ahab's fast was an expression of a heart genuinely humbled. His fasting did not *earn* God's mercy. Rather, it was an outward channel for expressing a heart that received God's humbling word against his sin. Ahab put on sackcloth, and went without food, to own the seriousness of his offense against God and to demonstrate a heart of repentance. And God saw that and honored it—for even such a one as Ahab—revealing a wideness and readiness in his mercy that should inspire us to fast, even today.

Fast in Three Directions

In addition to 1 Kings 21, three other passages explicitly link fasting and self-humbling. The first, Psalm 69:10, has *an inward focus or orientation*, like Ahab's fast: to express repentance. David says, "I wept and *humbled my soul with fasting.*" This is the most common and basic form of responsive fasting. God exposes, through his means, some grave or long-standing pattern of sin, and the ensuing fast expresses genuine sorrow for that sin, indiscretion, or error.

However, David's fast in Psalm 69 is not quite as simple as Ahab's. David's fast also could be an expression of grief over the ill-treatment he has received from his enemies, who made his sin (and fasting) an occasion to sin against him (Ps. 69:10–11). That's a second major category of fasting, with *an outward orientation*, grieving hard providences. Such a fast gives voice to mourning painful circumstances, as in the seven-day fast in Israel for the death of Saul (1 Chron. 10:12), or when Haman's edict arrived, threatening the lives of the Jews (Esther 4:3; see also Ps. 35:13–14; Ezra 9:2–5).

A third major category of fasting takes *a forward orientation*, seeking God's favor for a forthcoming endeavor. Before setting out from Babylon, Ezra proclaimed a fast "that we might *humble ourselves* before our God, *to seek from him a safe journey* for ourselves, our children, and all our goods" (Ezra 8:21). Here fasting serves as an intensifier alongside "forward" prayers for God's guidance, traveling mercies, and hand of favor. Ezra reports, "So we fasted and implored our God for this, and he listened to our entreaty" (v. 23). This kind of fasting forsakes self-reliance and admits our inability to produce or even predict the desired outcome (James 4:13–16).

Not So Fast

Finally, the fourth passage that links fasting and self-humbling is Isaiah 58:3–5, which sounds an important warning about what fasting is *not*.

The nation is in steep decline, and the people's hearts, by and large, are divided. Their devotion to God has become a shell, an outward show. They fast in an effort to manipulate God, rather than to express a humble heart—and God does not honor it.

They ask God, "Why have we fasted, and you see it not? Why have we *humbled ourselves*, and you take no knowledge of it?" (Isa. 58:3). God answers through his prophet,

> "Behold, in the day of your fast you seek your own pleasure. . . . Fasting like yours this day will not make your voice to be heard on high. Is such the fast that I choose, a day for a person to humble himself?" (Isa. 58:3–5)

In other words, your fasting is just a show to serve your sinful cravings, not the sincere expression of humble hearts. The external actions alone, apart from humility, are in vain. God will not be moved by such efforts. He sees the heart—as he did in Jesus' day, when Pharisees sought to turn fasting into self-exaltation (Matt. 6:16–18). The same still happens today.

Humble People Fast

Not everyone who fasts is humble. But humble people fast. They know themselves weak, and God strong. They know themselves small, and God big. They know themselves desperate, and God so ready to pounce with his great mercy. How can such people—humble people—not ask for his help, and not reach, at times, for that special prayer-intensifying tool he's given, precious and uncomfortable as it is, called fasting?

When we know that our God stands so ready to show mercy, like he did for such a wretch as Ahab, how can we not ask? Not only in daily prayer. And not only in scheduled fasts. But spontaneously.

> Not everyone who fasts is humble. But humble people fast.

Next time his humbling hand descends, what if you responded with prayer *and fasting*?

Chapter 7

Sell Yourself Short

I say to everyone among you
not to think of himself more highly
than he ought to think,
but to think with sober judgment.
Romans 12:3

We live in a day in which understatement is an endangered species. There is no shortage of embellishment and exaggeration. Public communication can sound like one grandiose sound bite after another. Parties, events, releases, contests, and political rallies must be bigger and better than the last.

In our society of hype and hyperbole, pomp and posturing, we embellish our online profiles, selecting our most flattering photo, highlighting our most impressive accomplishments, and filling our time-line with the confirming data, all carefully curated. We are enduring (not to overstate it) an epidemic of over-promising and under-performing. At least in the public eye, painfully few people seem to have the humility to speak, post, and report the simple truth.

Sadly, we often fall prey to this cultural pressure in Christian circles. This Sunday, this conference, this study, this book, this message must be more "epic" (talk about exaggeration) than the last. Such a penchant can be especially acute in church plant-ing and other ministry startups, when our collective insecurities and immaturities conspire to make it feel like everything needs to sound better than it actually is, to make us seem stronger than we truly are, to give the impression we have momentum and staying power. All the hype can amount to an elaborate and upbeat cover for feeling fragile, weak, and gnawingly uncertain.

But what if we unsubscribed from the madness? What if we asked ourselves, in such a world as ours, *How do I humble myself?*

Think Less of Yourself?

Wise men want to be humble. And yet, ironically, the first lesson we have learned in the pursuit of humility is that it's not something we can just up and do. The first step in seeking humility is a humbling one. Humility begins, as we've rehearsed again and again, with God's initiative, not ours.

However, even though self-humbling is beyond our control, God does give us the dignity of participating in the process, and the opportunity to prepare our hearts to *be humbled*. The apostle Paul, in one of the most important words in all the Bible about humility, gives us a glimpse into the kind of heart that is ready to receive God's humbling hand when it falls:

> I say to everyone among you *not to think of himself more highly than he ought to think, but to think with sober judgment*, each according to the measure of faith that God has assigned. (Rom. 12:3)

More than just guarding against swollen views of self, Paul would have us "think with sober judgment"—which means, among other things, don't spend a great deal of time thinking *about yourself*, your image, your achievements, your ability, your profile.

Yet self-awareness can be a mercy, even if Paul would caution us against self-*focus*. What might it mean, then, as a Christian, to *think with sober judgment* about self?

Observe the World's Pattern

First, we will do well to remember what kind of world we live in: one ballooned with inflated views of self. We cannot take our bearings from our surroundings and at the same time cultivate sober judgment of self. It is no accident that Paul writes in the immediately preceding verse, "*Do not be conformed to this world*, but be transformed by the

> We will do well to remember what kind of world we live in: one ballooned with inflated views of self.

renewal of your mind" (Rom. 12:2). It preached two millennia ago, and it still does today.

From the beginning, from humanity's very first sin, we have been overestimating ourselves. And as sin—the great, deadly, rebellious impulse in the creature to overestimate self in the face of his Creator—has taken root, and grown, and spread, and borne fruit in our world, one age after another (apart from revival) and has sought to outdo the others in self-regard.

Maybe modern humans are no more swollen with self-regard than our ancestors, but we do have a growing box of powerful digital tools for going into all the world and preaching ourselves. It's in the air. And on our screens.

If we look at the world around us for our balance, we will soar in self-exaltation or soon crash in self-pity.

We need to get our bearings before the face of God, with hearts daily and weekly recalibrated by the rhythms of God-focused worship and devotion. For most of us, the outworking of genuine humility before God will include a conscious and regular owning of our proneness to overestimate ourselves. Humility may feel like underestimating self because our age is so bent on overestimating. The goal is not to underestimate ourselves, though, but to *think with sober judgment*, and do so in the midst of a generation inebriated with self.

Choosing the Lowest Place

Jesus told a parable when he saw the evidence of such overestimation (pride) in wedding invitees. Rather than presuming to sit in "the place of honor," where you could get the best selfies, he instructed them instead,

> "Go and sit in the lowest place, so that when your host comes he may say to you, 'Friend, move up higher.' Then you will be honored in the presence of all who sit at table with you. For everyone who exalts himself will be humbled, and he who humbles him-self will be exalted." (Luke 14:10–11)

There it is again—humble yourself—and outside the book of 2 Chronicles, in the mouth of Jesus.

Christ would have his people think of themselves as ordinary, not special. As lowly, normal, one of the flock—not as a rabbi, teacher, instructor (Matt. 23:8–12). Not as a cut above the common man, but as happily ordinary, even gladly a servant. Even as a child (Matt. 18:3), as one who knows his smallness and dependence. Such people feel no need to pretend to be strong and self-sufficient; they are happily God-reliant and self-admittedly lowly, too modest to pretend otherwise.

Speak with Sober Judgment about Self

So, in Christ, we reject the world's pattern of self-exaltation and self-pity, but how will we discern what we really think about ourselves—and whether it is sober-minded or inflated? It will come out of our mouths.

Consider the countless junctures in everyday life when how we think about ourselves comes out for others to hear and see. How do you introduce yourself to a new face? How do you "tell your story," and what do you foreground? How polished a version of yourself do you put forward online? How often do your words—not to mention your social-media posts—slide into a humble-brag? Do you presume and anticipate public acknowledgment and appreciation from others? Do you deliberately self-denigrate, hoping someone will swoop in and correct you? Do you presume the greater seat, or happily (and quietly) head for the gallery?

Thinking with sober judgment may begin in our heads and hearts, but it comes out in due time. In our words. Spoken and written. Out there, cast in the world, for others to hear and see. And our words not only reveal our inner person, but also further shape our minds and hearts and who we will be tomorrow.

We Hunger for Humility

With our societal bent for overstatement and shameless hype, for facades, for smoke and mirrors, there is indeed a new hunger in our generation for humble, honest, Christ-exalting understatement. For modesty of speech.

We yearn for understatement, because there is so little access to it. The demand is rising, and the supply remains low. We ache for it from others—and yet we find ourselves frustratingly unable to produce it. Having been conditioned by the confetti of commercials, the posturing of politics, and the insecurities of social media, we cannot bring ourselves to do for others what we so desperately long for ourselves.

But we shouldn't be surprised that nonbelievers are left to deal in the counterfeit currency of endless exaggeration. Without Christ as the Great Security—the "surety," as the Puritans would say—how will we have the humility to leave our language at understatement?

Secure Enough to Be Small

It is humility, after all, that goes hand in hand with what we call "understatement."

Understatement, as a figure of speech, has long had the technical title "tapinosis," based on the Greek for humility (*tapeinosis*). It is humble to understate certain realities (especially when it comes to our own abilities and accomplishments) and allow others to experience the rare joy (almost inaccessible in modern life) of discovering something is *more* impressive than promised. And it's humble to understate ourselves such that some listeners may never know the full force of it—because we are secure enough in Christ to have our qualities go unacknowledged.

> We are secure enough in Christ to have our qualities go unacknowledged.

The Bible uses hyperbole at times as a literary device. But we are in a society so flooded with exaggeration, that understatement is what sticks out today as so countercultural, and so desperately needed—not just the surface expressions, but the humble heart that lies beneath them.

How refreshing to hear the psalmist pray, "A broken and contrite heart, O God, you will not despise" (Ps. 51:17). Not despise. Yes, that and so much more.

Or to hear the apostle Paul, doubtless one of the greatest to ever live, say in all sincerity, with manifest humility, "I am the least of the apostles, unworthy to be called an apostle" (1 Cor. 15:9). Then to enjoy this gospel summary, with honest self-deprecation: "Christ Jesus came into the world to save sinners, of whom I am the foremost" (1 Tim. 1:15). Or when he writes of "this light, momentary affliction" (2 Cor. 4:17), or asks his readers without any bombast and drama, "Brothers, pray for us" (1 Thess. 5:25).

Or perhaps most surprising of all to our modern ears—especially since the enterprising and exaggerating spirit seems to take hold of us deepest when we're part of some new work—Luke repeatedly describes the progress and impact of the early church in understated terms. When Peter was supernaturally delivered from prison, "there was no little disturbance among the soldiers" (Acts 12:18). When the gospel caused a riot in Ephesus, "there arose no little disturbance concerning the Way" (Acts 19:23). When Paul laid his hands on a young boy, and raised him from the dead, "they took the youth away alive, and were not a little comforted" (Acts 20:12; see also 14:27–28; 21:39; 27:20).

When Christ is our security, we learn to be content with our lives being more dramatic in reality than in our telling of them, whether online or in real conversation. Rather than making subtle, and sometimes shameless, efforts to have others think we're more impressive than we really are, we're happy to have them underestimate what otherwise might amaze.

Ultimately, it is the bigness and unsurpassed beauty of Christ, who is "the radiance of the glory of God" (Heb. 1:3), and whose worth we cannot overstate, that frees us from exaggeration and inspires us to understate self. As we're increasingly impressed with him, we lose that clawing, aching need inside to be impressed with ourselves, and press others in the service of helping us to believe it.

Chapter 8

He Humbled Himself

Behold, your king is coming to you . . .
humble and mounted on a donkey.
Zechariah 9:9

We have seen that God commands us to be humble. "Seek humility" (Zeph. 2:3). "Put on . . . humility" (Col. 3:12). "Have . . . a humble mind" (1 Pet. 3:8). "Clothe yourselves, all of you, with humility toward one another" (1 Pet. 5:5). Jesus' promise that God will exalt the humble enjoins us to pursue it (Matt. 18:4; 23:12; Luke 14:11; 18:14). And his apostles too say, "Humble yourselves" (James 4:10; 1 Pet. 5:6).

Yet humility, according to the regular testimony of Scripture, is not something we can just up and do.

As we considered the positive examples of those who humbled themselves (from Josiah and Hezekiah to Rehoboam, Ahab, and Manasseh)—as well as the negative examples of those who did not (Pharaoh, Zedekiah, Belshazzar)—what became clear is that humbling first belongs to the hand of God. He initiates the humbling of his creatures. And once he has, the question confronts us: Will you receive it? Will you humble yourself in response to his humbling hand, or will you kick against the goads?

"Humble yourselves," writes Peter, *"under the mighty hand of God"* (1 Pet. 5:6). First descends his humbling hand. Then the creature has his turn: *God is humbling me. Will I embrace it? Will I humble myself?*

Given this background, we now turn in this final chapter to the stunning portrayal of Christ in Phil. 2:8—in perhaps one of the most striking assertions in all the Scriptures: "he humbled himself." God himself, fully divine and fully human in the

> God himself, fully divine and fully human in the person of his Son, *humbled himself.*

person of his Son, *humbled himself*. This is worth our unhurried meditation and our endless marveling.

Humility Revisited

At the beginning of our study, in chapter 1, we briefly visited the first mention of humility in the Bible, in Moses' encounter with Pharaoh, and ventured a simple definition. Humility embraces the reality that *I am not God*. It is a posture of soul and body and life that acknowledges and welcomes the godness of God and the humanness of self.

We caught our first glimpse of this in the Bible's first mention of humility, when after seven plagues, God spoke to Pharaoh through Moses: "How long will you refuse to humble yourself before me?" (Exod. 10:3). Humility acknowledges and obeys the one who is truly God.

In chapter 1, we acknowledged that "Is God humble?" is a tricky question. Of course, God is not arrogant or prideful. He is not the *opposite* of what we would consider humble in a creature. However, we said, humility is a creaturely virtue, and he is

God—Creator, not creature. Now, we come to the conclusion that our study has been anticipating and awaiting all along: what makes us stand in awe as we read that the God-man, Jesus Christ, "humbled himself."

Christ Humbled Himself

Let's end our brief study in Scripture's self-humbling theme by marveling at this remarkable word from the apostle Paul—that Christ *"humbled himself"* (Phil. 2:8).

Note first, confirming our definition above of humility as a *creaturely virtue*, that the eternal Son *first* became man (v. 7), and only *then* humbled himself (v. 8). The verb Paul uses to capture the action of the incarnation is not *humbled* but *emptied*:

> [Being] in the form of God, [he] did not count equality with God a thing to be grasped, but *emptied himself*, by taking the form of a servant, being born in the likeness of men. (Phil. 2:6–7)

The movement from heaven to earth, so to speak, is an "emptying." The divine Son emptied himself not of divinity—as if that were possible—but of the privilege of not being human, not being a creature, not suffering the bounds and limitations of our finitude and the pains and afflictions of our fallen world. He could have "grasped" the divine privilege of not being subjected to the rules and realities of the creation, but instead "he emptied himself by taking" our humanity.

His was an emptying not by subtraction (of divinity) but by addition (of humanity): "taking."

By Becoming Obedient

So, first, he became man. Then, as man, came the creaturely virtue: "he humbled himself." Paul confirms in Philippians what we learned in Exodus 10 about humility in the negative example of Pharaoh:

> And being found in human form, he humbled himself *by becoming obedient* to the point of death, even death on a cross. (Phil. 2:8)

How did Jesus "humble himself"? *By becoming obedient.* To humble oneself is to acknowledge God as Lord and to obey as servant. In order to do so, then, the Son had to take "the form of a servant, being born in the likeness of men" (Phil. 2:7).

It is a mark of the fullness of his humanity, and his identification with us, that he didn't come on special terms, to be spared the frustrations of our limits and the pains of our world. Rather, he was all in: fully human in body, mind, heart, will, and surroundings. Fully human in our finitude and common frustrations. Fully human in our vulnerability to the worst a sinful world can work. Nor was he, at bottom, spared the very essence of being human: being accountable to God.

"Although he was a son," Hebrews 5:8–9 celebrates, "*he learned obedience* through what he suffered. And being made perfect, he became the source of eternal salvation to all who obey him." We, as creatures, must obey God—and he, as our brother, did the same.

To the Point of Death

But his self-humbling does not stop at obedience. The apostle adds, "to the point of death." Christ's obedience was an all-the-way obedience. A true and full obedience. He did not obey for a time, as long as it was comfortable, and then try another path. No, he obeyed *to the point of death*.

Genuine obedience *endures*. Christ did not begin in obedience and then surrender to disobedience once the greatest of threats loomed. He obeyed his parents (Luke 2:51), and obeyed his Father, in childhood, in adolescence, in adulthood, in Nazareth and Galilee, and all the way to Jerusalem. True obedience sees the word of God all the way through in our lives—both right away and for the long haul.

Humility not only obeys God as Lord, but continues to obey even as obedience mounts its increasing costs. It doesn't say, "I will obey for a time, until I've had enough, and then I'll fall back to my way." It says, "Your way, all the way, to the end, God." It begins in Galilee, sets its face like flint to Jerusalem, and in the garden, at the point of no return—even through sweat drops like blood—it trusts the Father, stays the course, and rises to meet its foes.

One more phrase then puts the exclamation point on Jesus' humility: "even death on a cross." Of all ends, his was the cruelest and most horrific: the Roman cross, emblem of suffering and shame. It's one thing to die; another to suffer torture; another still to be utterly shamed in the public eye as you are tortured to death.

And this obedience—this acknowledging and obeying his Father's word and will to the point of death, *even death on a cross*—is how Paul expands that most remarkable claim "he humbled himself."

Humbled with Him

God indeed does command our humility. His hand and plan conspire to humble us, whether through pandemics or the consequences of personal sins. And there in our humbling, whether our own sin played a part in it or not, he invites us to humble ourselves—and in no small measure by learning from the self-humbling of Christ.

The humility of Christ shows us that true humility is not the denigrating of humanity, but God's image shining in its fullness. To humble oneself is not to be less than human. Rather, it is pride that is the cancer, pride that corrodes our true dignity. To humble ourselves is to come ever closer, step by step, one degree at a time, to the bliss and full flourishing for which we were made.

The humility of Christ also clarifies that not all our humblings are owing to our own sin. Christ had no sin, yet humbled himself. Sometimes repentance is the first step in self-humbling; other times it is not. Our self-humblings may come in response to the exposure of our own sin, but not always. Humility welcomes the uncomfortable work of God whether it comes in clear response to our sin or not. Even Christ, sinless as he was, heeded the Father's call to humble himself.

> True humility is not the denigrating of humanity, but God's image shining in its fullness.

The humility of Christ also means God's command is not to something he himself has not experienced. As lonely as we may feel in our most humbling moments, we are not there alone. Christ has been there, and is there with us, fulfilling his pledge to be *with you always* (Matt. 28:20), and all the more tangibly when it's hardest. He humbled himself, and draws near in your humbling, to release you to receive it, welcome it, repent (if needed), declare his Father righteous, learn from it, and chart a new course with his guidance and presence, in his Word, in prayer, and among his people.

He Will Lift You Up

The humility of Christ, in his life and death and resurrection, testifies to one of God's clearest and most memorable promises in all the Scriptures: *he humbles the proud and exalts the humble.* So it was with Christ. He humbled himself, and "God has highly exalted him" (Phil. 2:9)—literally, "super-exalted" (Greek *hyperypsōsen*). And so too will our God, without exception, exalt those who are his in Christ. It is only a question of timing.

No matter how deep your valley, no matter how long it feels like you've been left to rot in your humbling, no matter how alone you've felt, he will raise you. In Christ, you will be super-exalted, in time.

God's favor for the humble will shine forth. His rescuing grace will arrive. He will not leave his humbled unexalted, if his humbled cling to him.

So we conclude where we began, with the great promise of 1 Peter 5:6: "Humble yourselves, therefore, under the mighty hand of God so that at the proper time he may exalt you." In Christ, we have a great God and Sovereign. His hand is indeed mighty. And he is more committed to our eternal happiness than our temporal comforts. His humbling hand is not painless, but he is gracious. So we learn to welcome his uncomfortable work.

Thanks

I thank God for Marshall Segal, fellow teacher and editor at Desiring God, who had the idea for this book. I was tracking down the humble-self language and theme and trying to fit it into one article. Marshall had the presence of mind to take a step back. One article? How about eight? Maybe a short book? And thank you, Taylor Combs and B&H, for your interest in this project.

As one who feels a long way from home on my own journey toward humility, I remember particular names and faces when I think of the conscious moments and seasons of being humbled and first learning to battle my own pride. For eighteen years, I lived in the home of a modest and genuinely humble man, my own father. And Mom too. They still love understatement.

humbled

In my college years, two older brothers gave energy to disciple me and saw more tears than anyone else: first Faamata Fonoimoana, then Matt Lorish. When I came to Minnesota, Paul Poteat and Matt Reagan were there for my most humbling of moments. In recent years, it's been Michael Thiel, Jonathan Parnell, and Joe Rigney. Thank you, dear brothers, for being there for me when the Humbling Hand descended.

In the day-in, day-out rhythms of the Teaching Team at Desiring God, I am regularly humbled by the remarkable abilities and humility of my colleagues, and their intellect and Christian EQ. In addition to Marshall, thank you, Scott Hubbard, Greg Morse, Jon Bloom, John Piper, and the Leadership Team.

Under Christ, the greatest human instrument of God's humbling work in my life has also been the most precious. We're going on fifteen years of marriage. There have been many uncomfortable and unpleasant humbling moments. But Megan has taught me to welcome them, not just by the grace she embodies but even by her kindness in those moments of correction. Often more kind than I'm able to see at first. And then time tells.

Scripture Index

Name and Subject Index

desiringGod

Everyone wants to be happy. Our website was born and built for happiness. We want people everywhere to understand and embrace the truth that *God is most glorified in us when we are most satisfied in him.* We've collected more than thirty years of John Piper's speaking and writing, including translations into more that thirty languages. We also provide a daily stream of new written, audio, and video resources to help you find the truth, purpose, and satisfaction that never end. And it's all available free of charge, thanks to the generosity of people who've been blessed by the ministry.

If you want more resources for true happiness, or if you want to learn more about our work at Desiring God, we invite you to visit us at **desiringGod.org.**